# Putting Nature in Focus
## One Picture and One Poem at a Time

### Debbie R. Hudson
Writer and Photographer

# Parson's Porch Books
www.parsonsporchbooks.com

*Putting Nature in Focus: One Picture and One Poem at a Time*
ISBN: Softcover 978-1-951472-00-9
Copyright © 2019 by Debbie R. Hudson

All rights reserved. No part of this book may be reproduced or transmitted in any form or by any means, electronic or mechanical, including photocopying, recording, or by any information storage and retrieval system, without permission in writing from the publisher.

Disclaimer: All photos were taken by Debbie R. Hudson. All Haiku and Poetry written solely by Debbie R. Hudson. None of which are to be copied, duplicated or used without permission.

*Putting Nature in Focus*

# Contents

Preface ............................................................................................... 7
Dedication ......................................................................................... 9
PINK ROSE ..................................................................................... 10
HONEYSUCKLE ............................................................................ 12
MOTH ............................................................................................. 14
YELLOW JACKET .......................................................................... 16
DOODLEBUG ................................................................................. 18
DAISY BLOOMS ............................................................................. 20
LILAC GRANDEUR ....................................................................... 22
DANDELION .................................................................................. 24
DAISY PETALS ............................................................................... 26
RED BIRD ....................................................................................... 28
BEAUTIFUL DAY ........................................................................... 30
PURPLE HUES ............................................................................... 32
VISION IN GREEN ........................................................................ 34
BESSIE BUG ................................................................................... 36
RED ROSE ...................................................................................... 38
GOD'S ARTWORK ......................................................................... 40
THE MAGNOLIA ........................................................................... 42
NATURE ERUPTS .......................................................................... 44
DAYLILY .......................................................................................... 46
COLORFUL BOUQUET ................................................................ 48
GARDEN SPIDER .......................................................................... 50
BLACKBERRY WINTER ................................................................ 52
NOT THE END .............................................................................. 54
COW or VOW? ............................................................................... 56
SPRY BUTTERFLY .......................................................................... 58

| | |
|---|---|
| BEES POLLINATE | 60 |
| SUN AND CLOUDS | 62 |
| GEORGIA PEACH | 64 |
| THE DUCK | 66 |
| RUDBECKIA | 68 |
| GRANDDADDY LONGLEGS | 70 |
| BUDS BURST | 72 |
| BLUE HYDRANGEA | 74 |
| SWEET SHRUB | 76 |
| PINCUSHION FLOWER | 78 |
| ZINNIA | 80 |
| OPEN YOUR EYES | 82 |
| DRAGONFLY | 84 |
| RED SPIDER LILY | 86 |
| HONEY-BEE | 88 |
| MORE THAN A WEED | 90 |
| ALL THINGS | 92 |
| JULY FLY | 94 |
| OPOSSUM | 96 |
| SUMMER SUN | 98 |
| SERINE STREAM | 100 |
| GREY FOX | 102 |
| ALLURING AZALEA | 104 |
| MAJESTIC BUTTERFLY | 106 |
| GOOSE DOWN | 108 |
| LANTANA | 110 |
| GO EXPLORE | 112 |
| MY INSPIRATION | 114 |

# Preface

As a single mother of two boys whom are eighteen years apart in age, and with the youngest of the two heading off to college in the fall of 2019, I knew I would need to find something to occupy my time. My home was soon, surely to be too quiet. Thus, my reason to start writing Haiku and Poetry. My uncle Dwayne Cole whom is an author of many books himself, suggested to me and advised that my poetry would go beautifully along with the many pictures I take. My love for taking pictures began soon after I got my first mobile phone with a camera. Let's just say, from that point on; I was hooked. Now my phone is rarely used for anything other than the camera. Though I take many pictures of my family, friends and my fur babies, I prefer to take pictures of all things in nature and some architecture. I feel as though the camera lens sometimes will capture what our eyes their self may miss at first glance. As I go back and look at the pictures I have taken, I realize how each aspect of nature has so many qualities to explore. For example, you may look a picture of a rock one day and see a hard and lifeless object sitting in the ground just waiting for you to step on it the wrong way and twist your ankle. Another day, you may look at that same picture of the rock sitting there and imagine just how many raindrops have fallen onto it and shaped it into the shape it is today. Then one day you may look at it and wonder, has this rock ever been used by someone to play a game or to fend off predators? As nature is so complex, so is our minds…use your mind and explore! Let it take you onto a beautiful adventure as I have. My hope is that as you read my first book and look at the pictures you too will go on an adventure. My desire is to follow with many more.

# Dedication

I hereby dedicate this book to my family for always being there for me when times were tough and for loving me unconditionally though it all!

Parents: Wendell and Brenda Cole
Oldest Son and Daughter-in-law: Brandon Baker and Amanda
Youngest Son: Mason Hudson- Thank you, Mason for proofing this book!
Grandchildren: Lane, Paige, Lorelai and Isaac
Fur-baby: Lucy Mae

In loving memory of my Grandparents:
Walter Lee Henderson and Mary Faye "Brock" Henderson
Robert Lewis Cole and Jessie Pearl "Stamps" Cole

# PINK ROSE

Pink rose so fragrant...
Petals soft like fresh spun silk!
Nature's enticement!

# HONEYSUCKLE

Sweet honeysuckle...
A fragrance undeniable!
Springs tasty delight!

# MOTH

Spread your airy lil wings...
Fly like a moth to a flame!
Nature's chemistry!

# YELLOW JACKET

Yellow jacket queen...
Yellow and black predator!
Majestic stinger!

# DOODLEBUG

Come sit in the dirt...
Get a stick, twirl it around!
Doodlebugs in the ground!

# DAISY BLOOMS

Blooms of a daisy…
White petals like silk so pure!
Natural breathtaking allure!

# LILAC GRANDEUR

A sight to behold…
Clusters of smalls lilac blooms.
Bouquet of grandeur!

# DANDELION

Pirouette dancer…
Such masters of survival!
Beneficial herb!

# **DAISY PETALS**

He loves me, or not?
Daisy petals bright as day!
Romance? Take a chance!

# RED BIRD

Songs so beautiful!
Leaves of green where red bird sings…
Loved ones are so near.

This Haiku was previously published in
*Down on the Farm in Georgia: A Poetical Memoir* by Dwayne Cole

# BEAUTIFUL DAY

As the sun shines bright,
Butterflies go in search of a delight!

As the gentle wind blows,
The petals being to sway!

Wind won't keep the butterfly away,
Not on this beautiful day!

As day turns into night,
Yellow wings shimmer in the light!

With the transformation of the day,
Let us all pray!

Pray that tomorrow will be,
Another beautiful day!

# PURPLE HUES

Pleasing purple hues…
Standing so gracefully tall!
Natures elegance!

# VISION IN GREEN

A vision in green!
Like fresh leaves in the spring…
Tugs on our heart strings!

# BESSIE BUG

Oh dear! Bessie bug!
Beetle so shiny and black...
Go home to your log!

# RED ROSE

Red rose so delicate…
Love will bloom and it may fade!
New buds will open soon!

# GOD'S ARTWORK

Artwork in the sky…
Sun and clouds varnished by God!
No comparison!

# THE MAGNOLIA

Symbol of the south!
Beetles and bees love these trees!
Alluring fragrance!

# NATURE ERUPTS

Beauty is abound…
Flowers erupt though the ground!
Nature's all around!

# DAYLILY

Look deep down inside...
If only for just for one day!
Beauty is within!

# COLORFUL BOUQUET

Flamboyant Bouquet…
It's like candy for your eyes!
Colors United!

# GARDEN SPIDER

Silk webs they do weave…
Without fear, they zig and zag!
Good Garden Spider!

# BLACKBERRY WINTER

Blackberry winter…
A chill in the morning air!
Yum, a warm cobbler!

# NOT THE END

Sometimes when things happen…
We don't understand why!

All we can do is cry!
Dry your tears my friend…

God has a plan!
This is not the end!

God don't put anything on us…
That we can't bear!

He needed your friend there!
Keep your memories within…

Until you meet again!
He is forever your best friend!

# COW or VOW?

Oh, what will I do?
Wendell knew he better think this one through
Daddy said the cow is sick,
Son it's up to you to see it through!
Oh, what will I do?
There's this girl I met at school,
She's so pretty and oh so cool!
We have a date, I must break.
I know what I must do!
I have a duty to follow through…
The cow gets me now,
Brenda gets me with a vow!

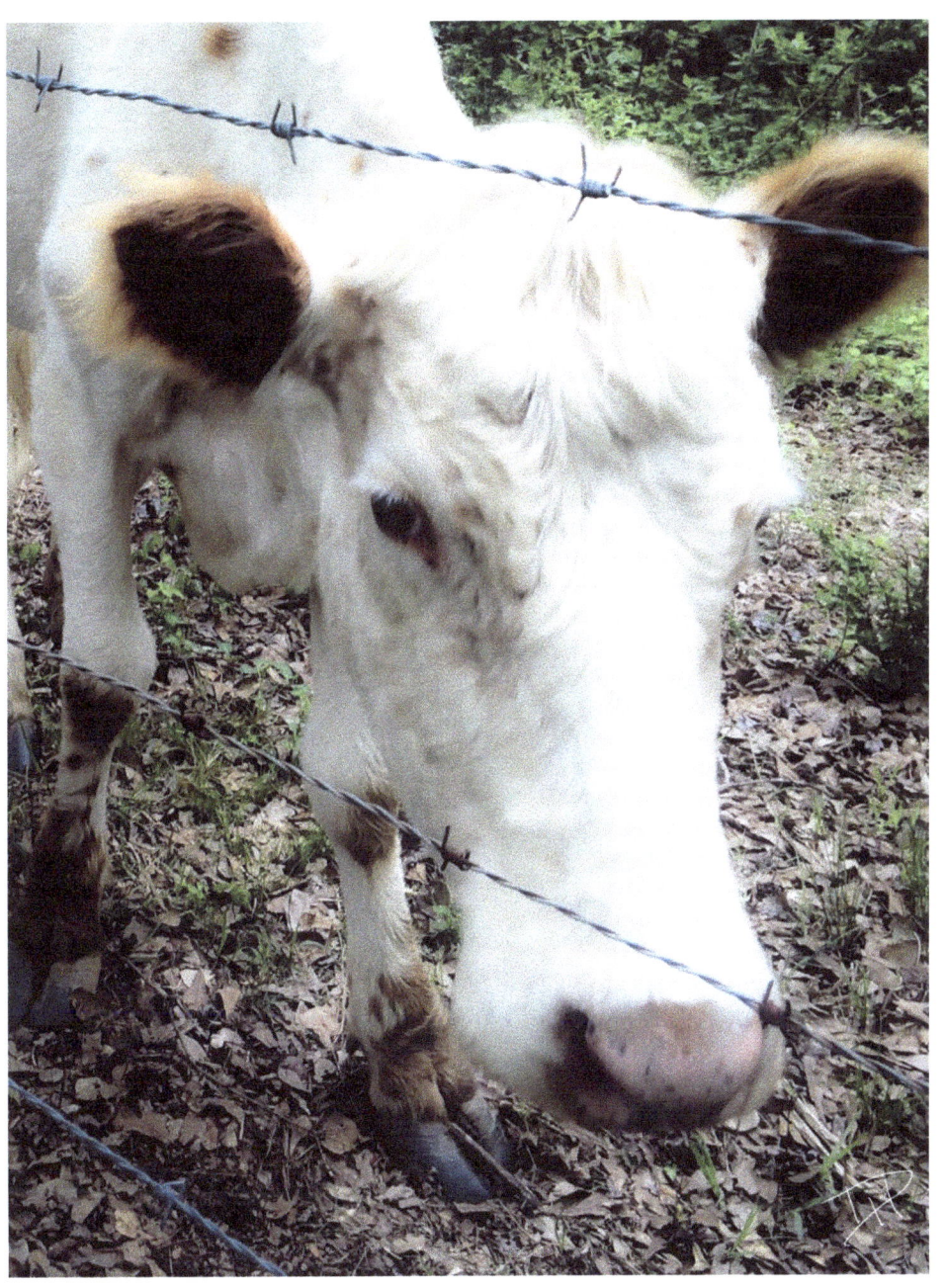

# SPRY BUTTERFLY

Butterfly so spry...
Lovely vision for my eyes!
Nature's transformer!

# BEES POLLINATE

Azaleas bees love!
Pollinate from dawn to dusk!
Agriculture pro!

## SUN AND CLOUDS

Sun I see today...
Tomorrow, clouds of dark gray!
Mother Nature's roused!

# GEORGIA PEACH

Sun ripe Georgia peach...
Fuzzy, fragrant fruit so sweet!
Natures juicy treat!

# THE DUCK

Can I please be fed?
All I ask is for some bread!
To the lake she sped!

# RUDBECKIA

Golden elegance...
Highlighted by the sunshine!
Blooms bright as the day!

# GRANDDADDY LONGLEGS

Creeping and crawling…
Granddaddy long legs he is!
Natures harvestmen!

# BUDS BURST

Tiny buds emerge…
Beauty bursts from deep within!
Full blooms, mesmerize!

# BLUE HYDRANGEA

My heart feels so blue…
Dear Granny, I still miss you!
Hydrangea you grew!

# SWEET SHRUB

Such sweet redolence…
Enticing blooms of maroon!
Aromatic shrub!

# PINCUSHION FLOWER

So airy like lace…
Dainty purple powerhouse!
Butterflies delight!

# ZINNIA

Bedazzling Zinnia…
Floral enchantment all spring!
Pink with stalks of green!

## OPEN YOUR EYES

A walk through the garden…
Brings joy to your soul!
The warmth of the sun…
Brings comfort within!
Nature has so much to offer…
Just open your eyes and take it in!
Relax and enjoy the beauty all around…
Happiness is there waiting to be found!
God put this all here…
For us all to enjoy!

# DRAGONFLY

Wings like sheer stained glass…
Fly swiftly, hover about!
Bring luck, Dragonfly!

# RED SPIDER LILY

Like fireworks in July…
Bright red spider lilies pop!
Floral explosion!

# HONEY-BEE

A bee do I see…
Workers gather sweet nectar!
Vital Honeybee!

# MORE THAN A WEED

Some may see a weed…
Dandelions are so much more!
Backyard useful herb!

# ALL THINGS

Late in the evening, just before night…
You may see things, that give you a fright!
Some may creep, some may crawl,
Some things are even really small!
Nature has it all!
Things that howl, things that hop…
And some things that will bring you to a stop
Some things are just a beautiful sight!
No matter if its day or night…
God made all things, just right!

# JULY FLY

Uninhibited...
Brilliant music radiates!
Vocal July fly!

# OPOSSUM

Beneficial? Yes!
Opossum eats ticks all day!
Don't go away! Stay!

# SUMMER SUN

Soaking up the sun...
Fur babies, flowers and rays!
Lazy summer day!

# SERINE STREAM

What better way,
To enjoy the day?
By the steam,
So pure and serine!
Get your feet wet,
Wash away the sweat!
Before you have to go,
Sit back, watch the water flow!
Nature's beauty never gets old!
It brings comfort to your soul!
Gods creations...
Much prettier than gold!

# GREY FOX

Beautiful creature!
Grey fox, not a rabbit's friend!
Stay out of my den!

# ALLURING AZALEA

Small bugs delight!
Pink azaleas attract all!
Poisonous allure!

# MAJESTIC BUTTERFLY

Fluttering about…
Vibrant wings so regal like!
Majestic monarch!

# GOOSE DOWN

Orange beak and feet...
Join the goose down by the creek!
A summer retreat!

# LANTANA

Cosmic Firestorm!
Beauty no one can deny!
Butterfly magnet!

# GO EXPLORE

Get out in nature...
Beauty is there to enjoy!
Enhance and explore!

# MY INSPIRATION

My inspiration?
Family, friends and flowers…
The fruits of my faith!


Blessings y'all!

*Debbie* :)

www.ingramcontent.com/pod-product-compliance
Lightning Source LLC
Chambersburg PA
CBHW041318110526
44591CB00021B/2834